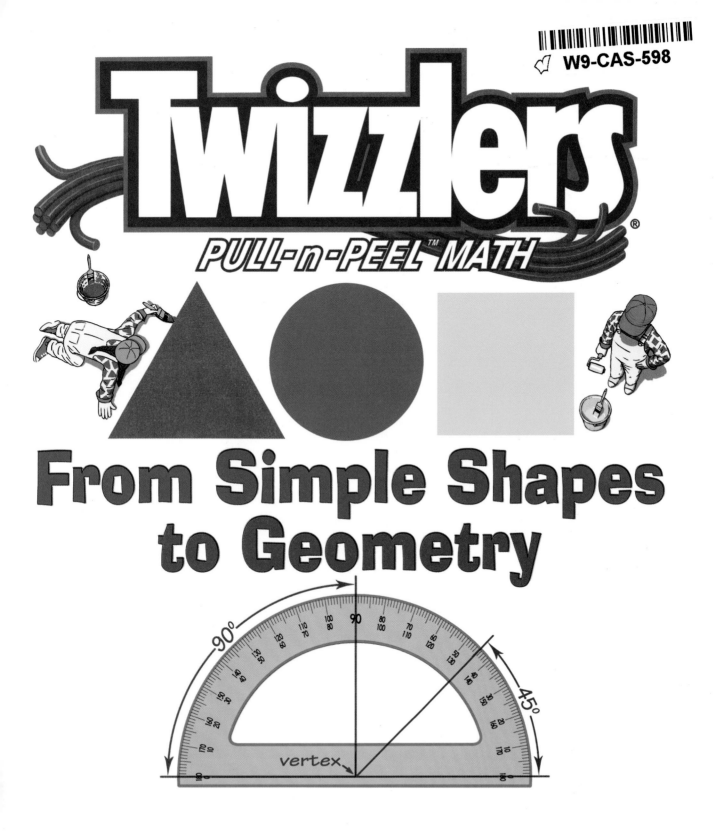

Twizzlers

PULL-n-PEEL™ MATH

From Simple Shapes to Geometry

90° 90 45° vertex

by Jerry Pallotta   Illustrated by Rob Bolster

SCHOLASTIC INC.

New York   Toronto   London   Auckland   Sydney   Mexico City   New Delhi   Hong Kong   Buenos Aires

Thank you to Karen and Michael Spencer.
—— Jerry Pallotta

This book is dedicated to my friend "Crunch."
—— Rob Bolster

ISBN 0-439-63992-1

12 11 10 9 8 7 6 5 4 3 2 1   5 6 7 8 9 10/0

Printed in the U.S.A.
First printing, October 2005

SIMPLE SHAPES

Here are some simple shapes.

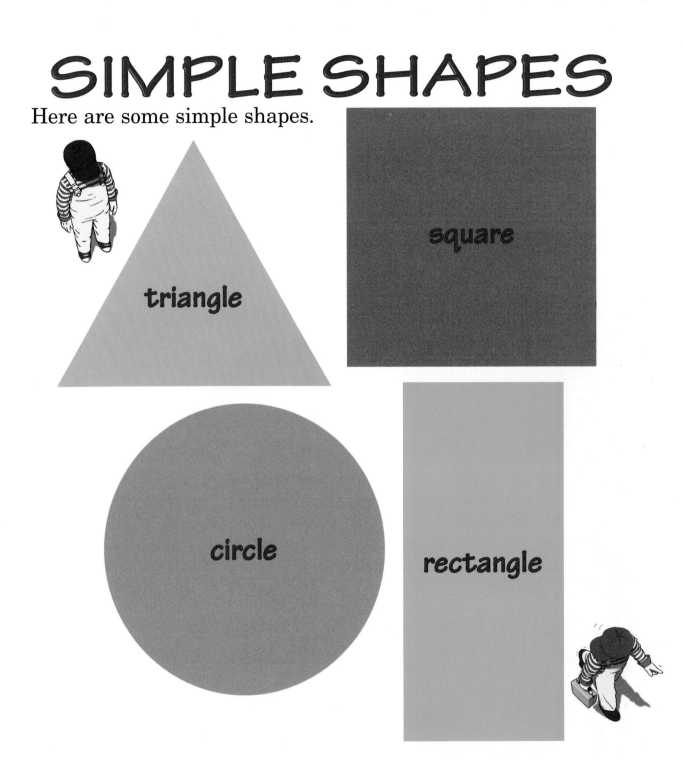

triangle

square

circle

rectangle

How did we make these simple shapes?
And what will help us make many other shapes?
We need to learn about points, lines, and angles.
So, let's go!

Start with a package of
TWIZZLERS® *PULL-n-PEEL*™ candy.

Cherry flavored will be fine.
Open it and pull out one piece.

4

It comes in a cable with nine strands.
Peel off one strand.
Don't eat it yet!

We will use it later as an example of a straight line.

PLANE

We need a place to put the points,
the lines, and the angles.
We need a plane.
No, not an airplane!
In math, a plane is a flat or level surface.
Pretend this page is not a sheet of paper.
Instead, imagine it is a level plane.

POINT

Now we'll draw a dot.

We will call it a point in space.
This point is not in outer space!
It is on our level plane.

Then we'll draw another point.

LINE

Now it's time to make a straight line.
Place a strand of **TWIZZLERS®** *PULL-n-PEEL*™ candy
between the two points.
This is called a line segment.

MORE LINES

ray

point

A line that goes on forever
from one point is called a ray.

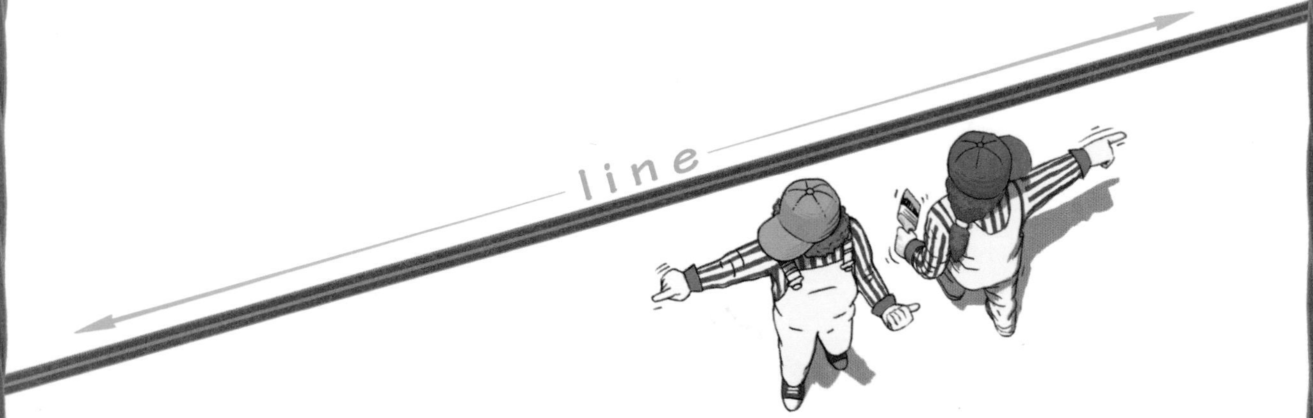

line

A line that goes on forever in both directions is called a line.

intersection
point

When two lines on the same plane
cross each other, they make a point.

ANGLE

Now let's draw some angles.
When two rays meet at a common point, they form an angle.

obtuse angle

Wide angles are called
obtuse angles.

acute angle

Skinny angles are called
acute angles.

straight angle

point →

A straight line is also known as a straight angle.

We are learning geometry!
Geometry is the study of planes, points, lines, angles, and shapes.

PARALLEL

Two straight lines that lie in the same plane and do not touch each other are called parallel lines.

Here are some!

Use your imagination and think of other parallel lines.
How about train tracks?
How about the lined paper in your notebooks or the lines on a football field?

RIGHT ANGLE

A "ninety-degree" angle is called a right angle.
The corner of this book is a right angle.
We will learn about degrees later.

$$\begin{array}{r} 90° \\ 90° \\ 90° \\ +\ 90° \\ \hline 360° \end{array}$$

SQUARE

Remember the simple shapes at the beginning of this book?

Now that you know about parallel lines and right angles,
you can make a square!
A square is a four-sided shape.
It has four line segments of equal length and four right angles.
The opposite sides of a square are parallel.

PERPENDICULAR

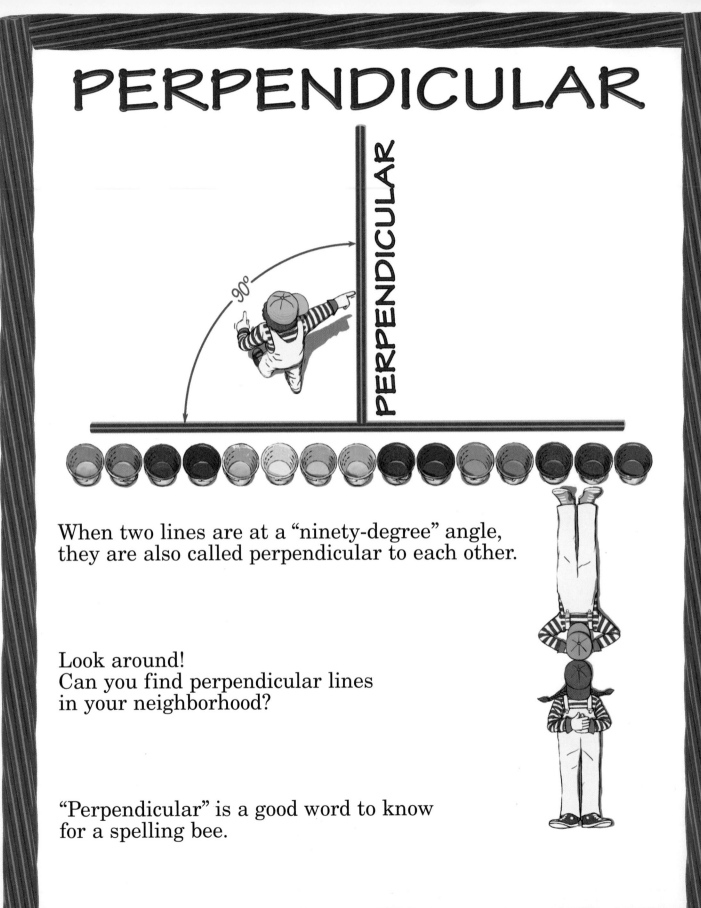

When two lines are at a "ninety-degree" angle, they are also called perpendicular to each other.

Look around!
Can you find perpendicular lines in your neighborhood?

"Perpendicular" is a good word to know for a spelling bee.

RECTANGLE

length

width

90°

90°

90°

90°

A rectangle is a shape that has four right angles and four sides.
Opposite sides are parallel and have the same length.
The perpendicular sides are a different length.

PERIMETER

Here is a new term to learn: perimeter!
It is the distance around a shape.

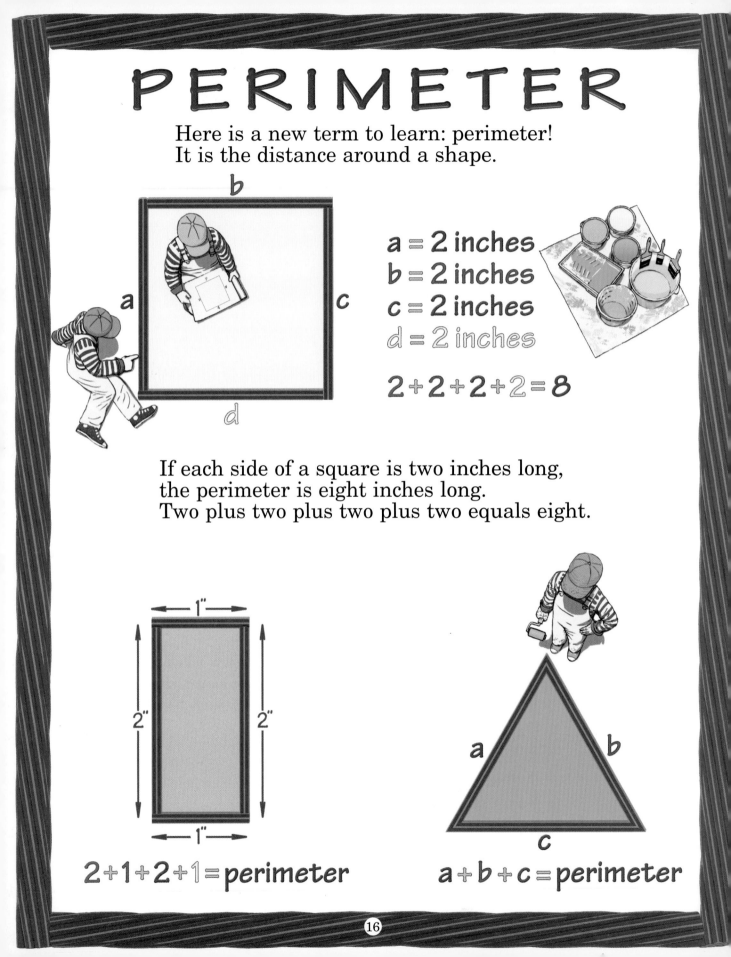

$a = 2$ inches
$b = 2$ inches
$c = 2$ inches
$d = 2$ inches

$2 + 2 + 2 + 2 = 8$

If each side of a square is two inches long,
the perimeter is eight inches long.
Two plus two plus two plus two equals eight.

$2 + 1 + 2 + 1 = $ perimeter

$a + b + c = $ perimeter

FORMULA

This is the formula for finding the perimeter of a shape.

$$a+b+c+d=PERIMETER$$

Count the sides.
Measure the length of each side.
Then add up the lengths of all the sides.

b

a = 2 inches
b = 5 inches
c = 2 inches
d = 5 inches

2+5+2+5=14 inches

a

c

d

This rectangle is five inches long and two inches wide.
Two plus five plus two plus five equals fourteen.

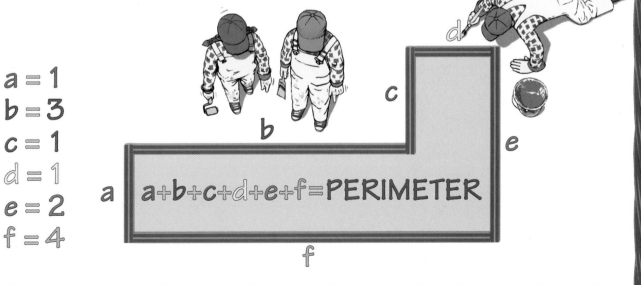

a = 1
b = 3
c = 1
d = 1
e = 2
f = 4

c

b

e

a   a+b+c+d+e+f=PERIMETER

f

One plus three plus one plus one plus two plus four equals twelve.

AREA

2"

We measure a line by its length.

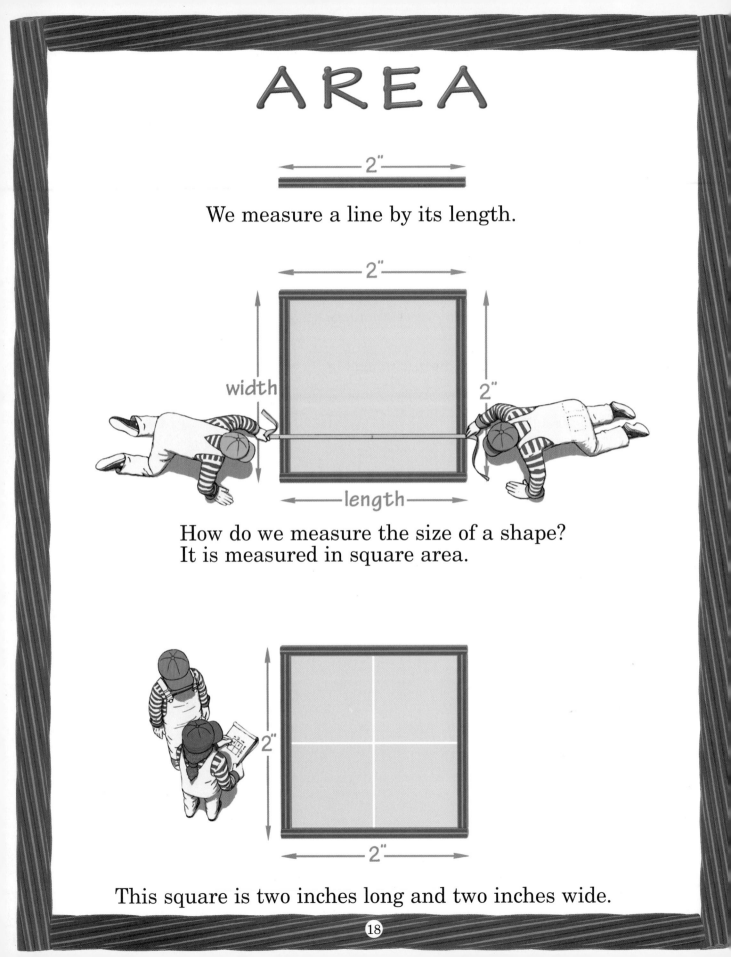

2"

width

2"

length

How do we measure the size of a shape?
It is measured in square area.

2"

2"

This square is two inches long and two inches wide.

FORMULA

This is the formula for finding the square area of a shape.

length × width = square area

This is not a secret formula!

Measure the length.
Measure the width.
Length times width equals square area.

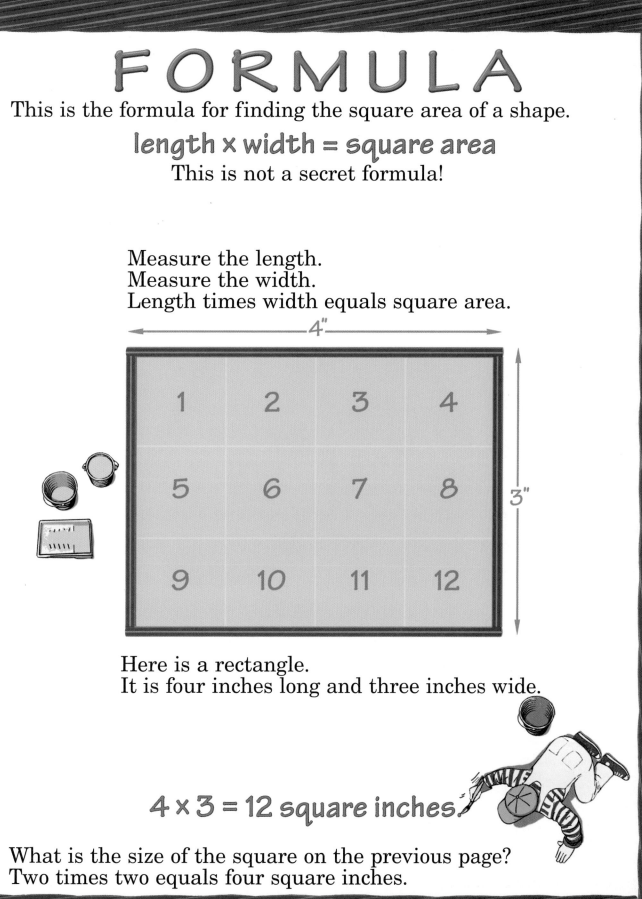

Here is a rectangle.
It is four inches long and three inches wide.

4 × 3 = 12 square inches.

What is the size of the square on the previous page?
Two times two equals four square inches.

TRIANGLE

Now let's make another simple shape.
A triangle is made with three lines and three angles.

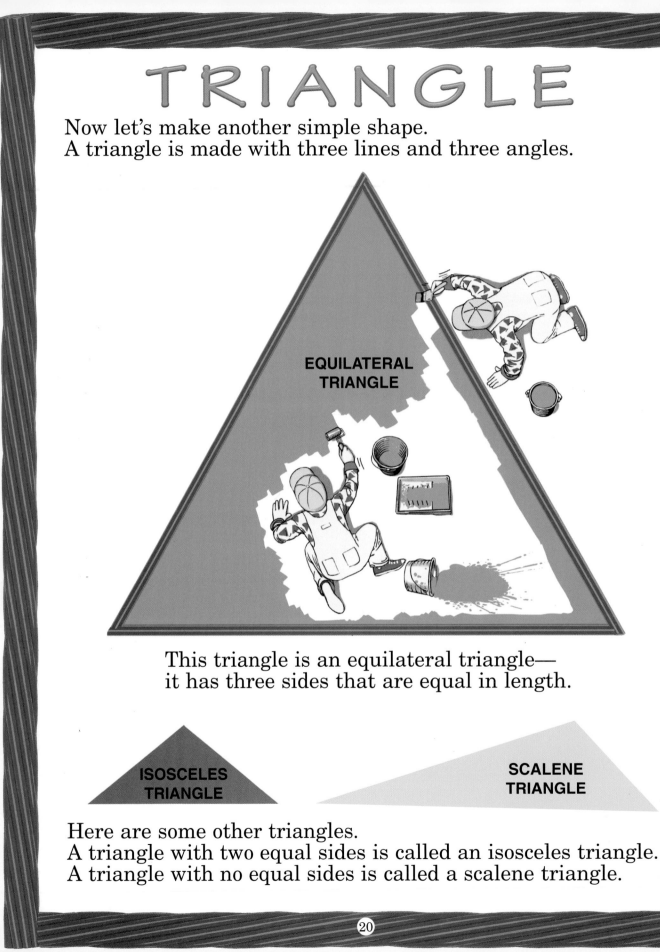

EQUILATERAL
TRIANGLE

This triangle is an equilateral triangle—
it has three sides that are equal in length.

ISOSCELES
TRIANGLE

SCALENE
TRIANGLE

Here are some other triangles.
A triangle with two equal sides is called an isosceles triangle.
A triangle with no equal sides is called a scalene triangle.

VERTEX

What did one ray say to the other ray? "Let's meet!"

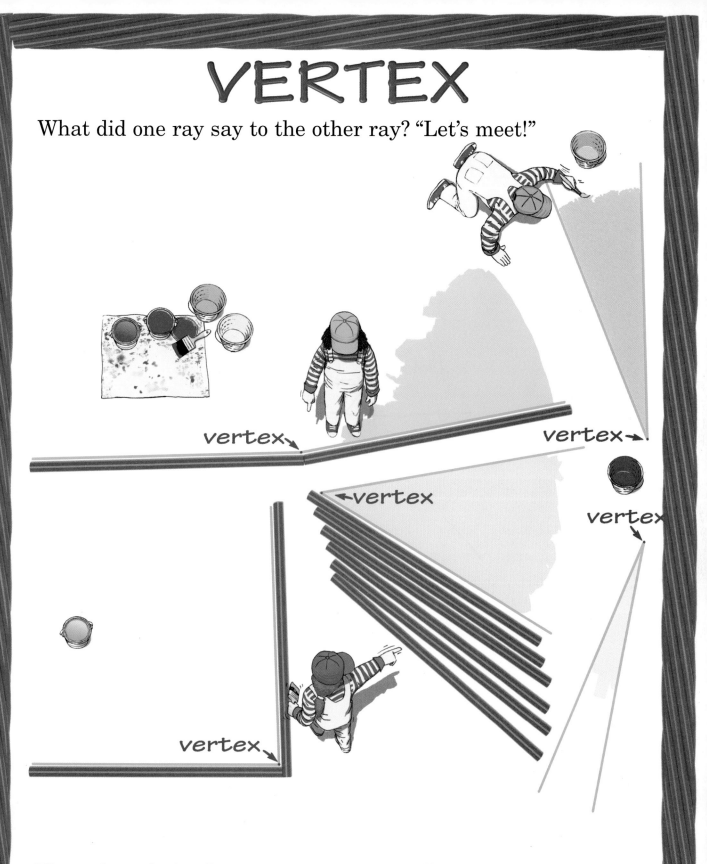

The point where the two rays meet is called the vertex.

CIRCLE

Let's make another simple shape.
Draw a point.
Now put a curved line around the point.
If the distance between the center point and any point
on the curved line is the same, then this shape is a circle.

Here are some more circles.
One of them is squished.
But there is no such thing as a squished circle.
A squished circle is called an oval.

CIRCUMFERENCE

The distance around a circle is called the circumference.
Here are some more terms to learn about circles:
center, radius, diameter, and chord.

The shortest distance between the center point and the
circumference is called the radius.

Using a straight line, the distance from one point on the circle
through the center point to another point on the circle is called
the diameter.

A line between two points on the circle that does not go through
the center point is called a chord.

DEGREES

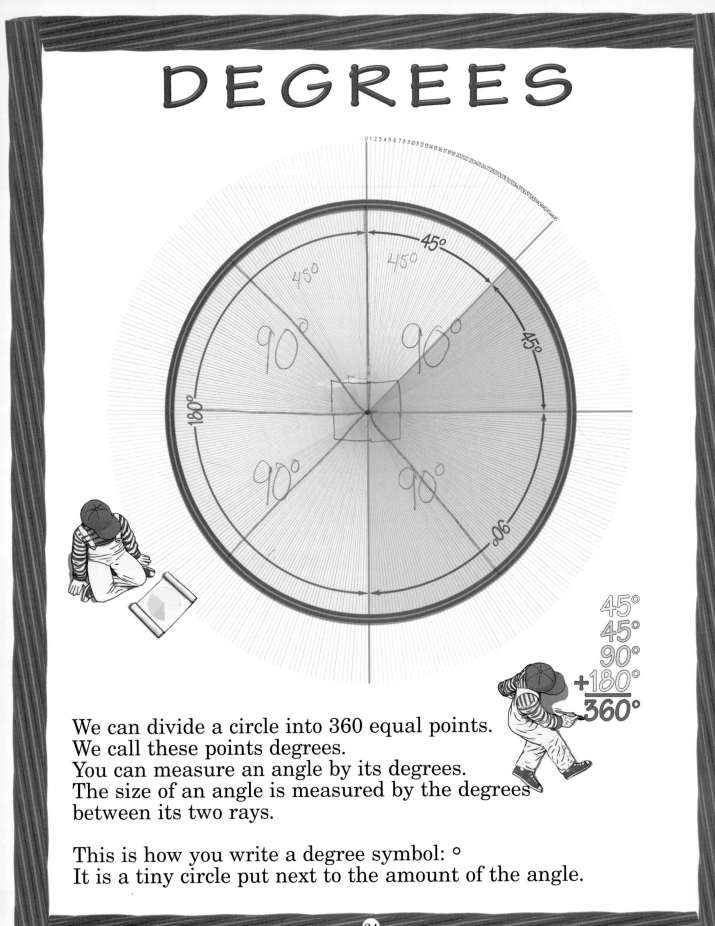

We can divide a circle into 360 equal points.
We call these points degrees.
You can measure an angle by its degrees.
The size of an angle is measured by the degrees
between its two rays.

This is how you write a degree symbol: °
It is a tiny circle put next to the amount of the angle.

PROTRACTOR

How do you know the size of an angle? You can measure it!
The tool that is used to measure an angle is called a protractor.
Angles that are less than ninety degrees are acute angles.
Angles that are greater than ninety degrees are obtuse angles.

CUBE

When studying geometry, we also learn about solid shapes. They have three dimensions—length, width, and height.

A cube has six flat sides.
Each side is the same size.
Each side is a square.
All edges have the same length.
The angles are at right angles.

SPHERE

A sphere is a three-dimensional circle.

It is easy to think of spheres that really exist.
There are baseballs, basketballs, gumballs,
the earth, and the moon.
Can you think of any other spheres?

PYRAMID

This pyramid is made with a square at the base and four triangles. Take a close look at it.

We can make another pyramid with a triangle as a base and three triangles as sides.
A pentagon could also be the base of a pyramid.
The famous Egyptian pyramids are made with square bases.

CONE

A cone is a three-dimensional shape that has a circle for a base.
It has a curved surface that rises up to one sharp point, the vertex!

The most common cone is an ice-cream cone.
Traffic cones block off cars from road repair work.
What other cones can you think of?

PRISM

A prism is a solid shape that has parallel ends that are the same size and shape.
This prism has a triangle on each end.
Between the parallel triangles, there are rectangles.

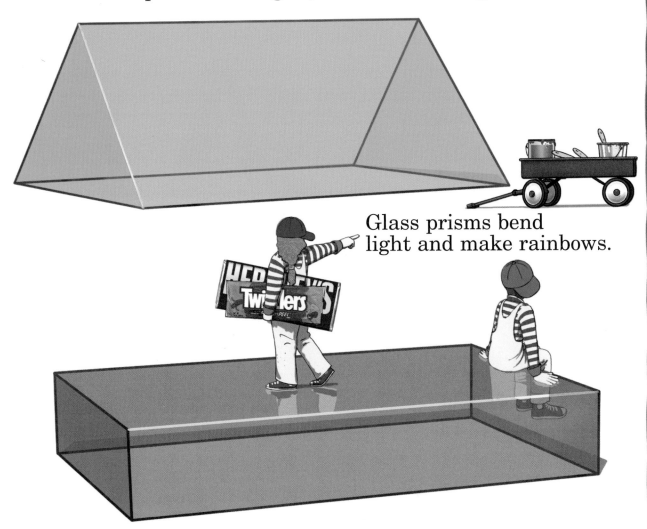

Glass prisms bend light and make rainbows.

This pink prism is a rectangular prism.

From now on, when looking at shapes,
you should think of math and geometry.
The shapes are made of points, lines, and angles.
You can look for parts that are parallel and perpendicular.
Shapes can be measured by length, width, height,
perimeter, and area.

CYLINDER

Geometry is all around us.

Here are eight cylinders.

Don't just look at these cylinders.
Think of them mathematically.
Do you see a circle? Are there right angles?
Can you find the diameter of each circle?

DIMENSION

Do you remember the difference between lines, simple shapes, and solid shapes?

This is a line segment.
It has one dimension: length.
It is one-dimensional.

This is a rectangle.
It has two dimensions:
length and width.
It is two-dimensional.

This is a cube.
It has three dimensions:
length, width, and height.
It is three-dimensional.